Content-Based Instruction

Content-Based Instruction

What Every ESL Teacher Needs to Know

Marguerite Ann Snow

and

Donna M. Brinton

University of Michigan Press
Ann Arbor

First paperback edition 2023

Published in the United States of America by the
University of Michigan Press

Paperback ISBN: 978-0-472-03957-9
Ebook ISBN: 978-0-472-12617-0

First published February 2019

CONTENTS

1. Overview of Content-Based Instruction

The integration of language and content has a long and distinguished tradition in second/foreign (SFL) language instruction. In fact, one of the earliest examples of such an integrated approach can be found in the Canadian immersion programs, which first appeared on the scene in North America in the early 1960s (Lambert & Tucker, 1972). In the immersion model, students receive the majority of their schooling through the medium of a second language (L2), basically studying their school subjects such as mathematics or science as they otherwise would, albeit in a foreign language (Snow, 2014). Today, immersion programs are recognized as being the earliest precursor of other types of content-based instruction (CBI). As we'll be discussing in this volume, the approach has evolved and adapted to a wide variety of educational settings, spawning new models of CBI in the process.

Defining Integrated Content and Language Instruction

Davison and Williams (2001) describe integrated language and content teaching as:

> ... a heuristic label for a diverse group of curriculum approaches which share a concern for facilitating language learning broadly defined, through varied but systematic linking of subject matter and language in the context of learning activities. (p. 57)

Further, Snow (2014) defines CBI as:

> ... an umbrella term for a multifaceted approach to SFL teaching that differs in terms of factors such as educational setting, program objectives, and target population but shares a common point of departure—the integration of language teaching aims with content instruction. (p. 439)

What these two definitions have in common are the following characteristics of CBI:

- It is an overarching approach to language teaching that takes into account diverse educational settings, program objectives, and target populations.
- Its primary aim is the integration or linking of language and content instruction.
- Through this linking, SFL learning is facilitated.

We can trace the impetus for CBI to the advent of communicative language teaching (CLT) in the 1970s, which was profoundly influenced by Hymes (1971) and others who proposed a more socially oriented approach to linguistics. The notion of "communicative competence" proposed by Hymes and his colleagues refers to the ability to use language effectively and appropriately in a variety of contexts. CLT formed a suitable backdrop to approaches such as the aforementioned immersion programs in Canada (Genesee, 1987; Tedick et al., 2011); other curricular approaches compatible with CLT such as CBI, English for Specific Purposes (ESP), English for Academic Purposes (EAP), and task-based language teaching (Duff, 2014); and the language across the curriculum movement in the U.K. and U.S. (*A language for life*, 1975; Parker, 1985)—all of which advocate, to some extent, for the integration of language and content teaching aims.

A Brief History

The first published volume on CBI appeared in 1986, with Bernard Mohan's aptly named volume *Language and Content*. In the introduction to the volume, Mohan exposed an underlying paradox in typical instructional settings when he noted, "In subject learning we overlook the role of language as a medium of instruction. In language learning we overlook the fact that content is being communicated" (p. 1).

Following closely on the heels of Mohan's volume, important groundwork for CBI began to be laid elsewhere in North America, with important centers of activity including the University of California, Los Angeles, the Monterey Institute of International Studies, the University of British Columbia, and the University of Ottawa. By the late 1980s, the modern language teaching community in the U.S. also began to apply CBI principles to "disciplined-based" approaches. Foreign languages across the curriculum programs sprang up at such places as St. Olaf College (Minnesota), the University of Minnesota, Eastern Michigan University, Earlham College (Indiana), and the University of Rhode Island (Krueger & Ryan, 1993). Since these beginnings, CBI has spread literally throughout the world, with the movement taking hold in both the English as a second language (ESL) and English as a foreign language (EFL) contexts. Increasingly today, it is being used in contexts where English functions as an international language of communication, or *lingua franca*.

Three Prototype Models of CBI

Another early work on CBI is that of Brinton and colleagues (1989). In it, the authors attempted to capture the three primary models of CBI that existed at the time: (a) theme-based instruction, (b) sheltered instruction, and (c) adjunct instruction. Recognizing that the approach needed to remain flexible, they identified these as "prototype" models, leaving room for practitioners to adapt the models to their own instructional contexts. Though today many additional models of CBI exist, these three models (see Figure 1.1) remain central to the approach.

Theme-Based Instruction

Theme-based instruction refers to instruction that focuses on specific themes of interest and relevance to the learners. These themes create the

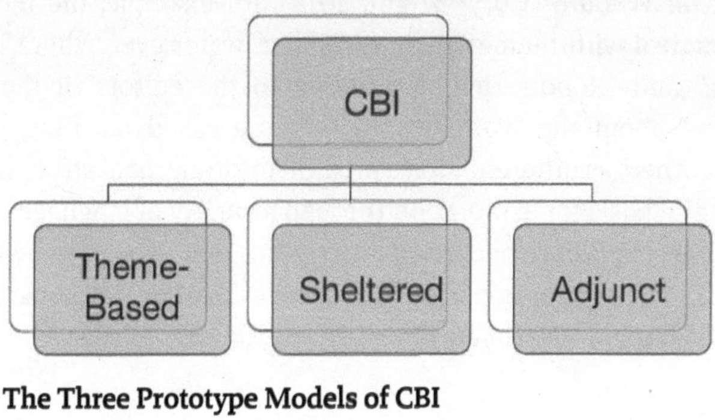

Figure 1.1: The Three Prototype Models of CBI

organizing principle for the course and provide the point of departure for skill- and language-based instruction. Themes can vary from a self-contained unit in the students' textbooks (see Example 1) to the extended or "sustained" treatment of content over several weeks or even an entire term (Murphy & Stoller, 2001) (see Example 2). The thematic texts and associated interactive tasks provide the language-rich environment that allows learners to acquire the L2.

Theme-based instruction is possible at virtually any level of instruction (from beginning to advanced), though probably most suitable for students at intermediate and higher language proficiency. It is also suitable for both younger learners and adults. To locate an example of theme-based instruction, one has only to look at the many multi-skills textbooks on the commercial market today that have adopted this approach as their organizing principle. Listed in the textbooks' table of contents are chapter titles such as "Extreme Sports," "Voluntourism," "Your Green Footprint," "Smart Cars," and the like. The course designer's challenge is to find suitable themes for the students in question and level-appropriate texts to provide input. An additional challenge is to determine the language and skill foci that are appropriate to cover in each thematic module and how to best integrate and sequence these items in the overall course.

Example 1: A Textbook Theme-Based Unit

Intended as a text for young learners, the National Geographic/Cengage Learning series *Our World* is organized around themes of high interest. In *Our World 6* (Cory-Wright, 2014), for example, the individual chapters deal with themes such as "Water, water everywhere," "Smart choices," and "Robots rule." According to the editors of the series, "Learning about the world through theme-based teaching benefits young learners as different topics provide informational structure and a meaningful basis for exploration through a variety of language learning tasks. Learning is enriched through activities that expand knowledge of the world and its people, places, and cultures" (https://ngl.cengage.com/ourworldtours/levels-1-6/ae/)

Example 2: A Teacher-Created Sustained Content Unit

Hauschild and colleagues (2012) report on a theme-based unit entitled "Going green," that merges a focus on environmental education with a focus on academic language preparation. Although designed for students enrolled in an academic preparation program, the unit can be adapted to a variety of levels and teaching contexts. The focus on environmental education teaches students how to contribute to a more sustainable environment and heightens students' interest in contemporary issues such as deforestation or water scarcity. Targeted tasks and authentic materials help to promote language acquisition and prepare students for meaningful communication. The four skills of listening, speaking, reading, and writing and an emphasis on critical thinking and autonomous learning are integrated throughout the unit.

Sheltered Instruction

The second model, **sheltered instruction**, refers to instructional models in which students who are still developing in their L2 proficiency are separated from native speakers for the purpose of content instruction, which is delivered in the students' L2. The original sheltered content courses were developed at the bilingual University of Ottawa where *Introduction to Psychology* was offered to non-native speakers of English and taught by a native English-speaking psychology professor; a separate section of *Introduction á la Psychologie* was offered to non-native speakers of French and taught by a French-speaking professor (Brinton et al., 1989). As an incentive for taking the course, students received unit credit for both the psychology course and foreign language (FL) credit. The professors in their respective courses were assisted by an English-or French-language instructor who spent about 15–20 minutes before each class reviewing the readings and preparing students for upcoming topics. Evaluation of the sheltered courses revealed that the sheltered L2 students made significant gains in both English and French, respectively, that were equal to or greater than the gains of students in well-taught ESL and French as a Second Language classes at comparable proficiency levels (Edwards et al., 1984; Hauptmann et al., 1988).

The sheltered model has since seen widespread implementation at the elementary and secondary levels in the U.S. and in some EFL settings (see Examples 3 and 4). The instructor is typically a content specialist, for example, a secondary school science teacher, who has specialized training in "sheltering" techniques, also referred to as "Specially Designed Academic Instruction in English" (Reynolds, 2015), for making the content comprehensible (e.g., via the use of visuals, pre-reading tasks, lexical accommodation, strategy instruction, and frequent comprehension checks). In this manner, instructors assist students with their language skill development and help them to access academically challenging content material. Exposure to rich academic language and complex concepts coupled with language-sensitive instructional delivery provide the necessary conditions for L2 acquisition to occur.

Those seeking guidance in implementing sheltered instruction are advised to consult the Sheltered Instruction Observation Protocol (SIOP) (Echevarría et al., 2017). SIOP is a comprehensive, field-tested model of sheltered instruction that specifies the features of high-quality sheltered lessons for teaching content to L2 students. The protocol has eight components including: (1) lesson preparation (e.g., designing content and language objectives); (2) building students' background knowledge; (3) comprehensible input; (4) instructional strategies; (5) interactional grouping configurations; (6) practice/application; (7) lesson delivery; and (8) review and assessment. SIOP offers an extensively researched tool for observing and quantifying a teacher's implementation of sheltered instruction. In a study of the academic literacy of secondary English learners (ELs) whose teachers had participated in professional development using the SIOP, ELs made significant gains in reading, writing, and oral proficiency compared to similar students whose teachers had not received SIOP training (Short et al., 2012).

Example 3: Sheltered Instruction at the Primary Level

An example of sheltered instruction at the primary level involves a sheltered science class where elementary school students in a bilingual program are engaged in a unit about the rainforest (U.S. Department of State, 2007). In the video accompanying the unit, we can see that one corner of the classroom is transformed into a rainforest, complete with improvised hanging vines and a rainforest canopy affixed to the ceiling. We can also see the teacher conducting a warm-up activity where students sing a song about the water cycle (to the tune of "Clementine");

the teacher then reviews and reinforces key vocabulary (adjectives, nouns, verbs, and adverbs) and guides the students to produce creative sentences about the creatures who live in the rainforest (e.g., "Big yellow jaguars fight madly on the ground," "Small poisonous monkeys scratch quickly in the canopy"). The class ends with students writing three sentences about rainforest creatures in their journals.

Example 4: Sheltered Instruction at the Secondary Level

Bright (2010) describes a ninth-grade sheltered mathematics class at a large suburban high school in Virginia, just outside of Washington, DC More than 20 percent of the school's population qualifies for English to Speakers of Other Languages (ESOL) services. Education at this school is standards-based, meaning that teachers are required to integrate national and/or district content standards into their instruction; the teacher of the sheltered math class is also certified in ESOL and builds active production and receptive understanding into the lesson. In her account, Bright describes ways in which the mathematics teacher creates a supportive learning environment for her L2 learners and encourages risk taking. By systematically foregrounding language issues in the mathematics curriculum, she helps students to acquire key vocabulary and to develop their academic register.

Adjunct Instruction

Finally, **adjunct instruction** refers to instructional models in which two courses (a content and language course) are paired, with the content and language instructors collaborating to merge (or dovetail) their instructional objectives. Often, L2 students in this CBI model are separated for the purpose of language instruction but combined with mainstream students in the content course. The content course typically provides the point of departure for decisions about what to teach in the language class; language objectives are identified with respect to students' linguistic needs in the content class. L2 acquisition occurs through exposure to high-level, challenging language in the content course and through the systematic academic language instruction provided in the language course (Brinton et al., 2003). This model offers students "two for one"—i.e., increased language proficiency as well as in-depth mastery of the content material. Examples 5 and 6 illustrate the use of this model in the U.S. and abroad.

Example 5: Adjunct Instruction at a U.S. University

A frequently cited example of adjunct instruction is UCLA's Freshman Summer Program, as described in *Content-Based Second Language Instruction* (Brinton et al., 2003). In this summer bridge program, first-year L2 students identified by university admissions as "high risk" take an EAP course paired with a content-area course that fulfills one of the students' general education requirements (for example, Introduction to Psychology). In collaboration with the content-area professor and their teaching assistants, the EAP instructors identify language objectives that can assist students in their reading and writing assignments for the content course. They also stress academic preparation skills with a view toward preparing students for the general demands of academia. In a study by Snow and Brinton (1988), former FSP students ranked the academic skills they learned (e.g., taking lecture notes, preparing reading guides, in-class essay/exam strategies) highly; however, above all, "adjusting to UCLA" was the highest-rated benefit of the adjunct experience.

Example 6: Adjunct Instruction at a Turkish University

An additional example of adjunct instruction involves an English/philosophy adjunct course offered at an English-medium private university in Turkey (Spring, 2010). In this instance, the adjunct course is part of a larger initiative at the university to enrich sophomore-level EAP classes. Students in their second year attend linked English and philosophy courses, with the language component organized around the philosophy topics and texts, which provides the point of departure for the language syllabus. The ultimate goal is to broaden students' intellectual background knowledge and cognitive skills and expose them to unabridged primary source texts.

Content-Driven vs. Language-Driven Models

Clearly, the three prototype models of CBI place differential amounts of emphasis on language and content. Met (1999) used the labels "content-driven" and "language-driven" to capture the varying degree of emphasis on language and content that underlies different CBI models. This difference is also captured by van Lier (2005) in his sliding scale of language and content (see Figure 1.2). Falling on the left-hand side of the scale (e.g., at Point A) are courses where "language takes precedence over content" (p. 16)—that is, in Met's analysis courses that are language-driven. On the right-hand side of the scale (e.g., at Point B) are courses where "content takes precedence over language" (p. 16)—that is, courses that Met would term content-driven. According to van Lier's analysis, theme-based courses (where the theme or content is a carrier topic for the language being presented and practiced) would thus fall at Point A on the continuum; sheltered courses (where mastery of content is primary and L2 development occurs through exposure to the contextualized language of the subject matter), on the other hand, would fall at Point B. Finally, at the mid-point on the scale, we could place adjunct instruction, where the two courses combined provide a balanced emphasis on both language and content.

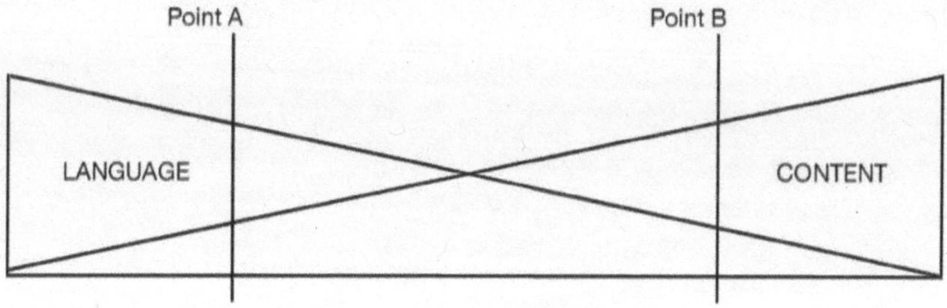

Figure 1.2: Van Lier's Scale of Language and Content
From Van Lier, L. (2005). The bellman's map: Avoiding the "perfect and absolute blank" in language learning. In Renée M. Jourdenais & Sarah E. Springer (Eds.), *Content, tasks and projects in the language classroom: 2004 conference proceedings* (pp. 13–22). Monterey, CA: Monterey Institute of International Studies. Used with permission.

Reflection

1. Three "prototype" models of CBI are outlined. Do you have experience with any of them? If so, what was this experience like?
2. What role does content play in your current teaching situation?
3. Given your student population, which themes or topics do you think would work particularly well? Why?
4. Does CBI seem appropriate for all levels of student proficiency? Why/why not?

2. Emergence of Additional Models of CBI

Surveying the landscape of CBI some 30 plus years after the appearance of Mohan's (1986) *Language and Content*, one cannot help but be struck by the variety of new and/or hybrid models of CBI. As predicted by Brinton and colleagues (1989), practitioners over the years have adapted the models to their own instructional contexts. This in turn has led to the proliferation of CBI models on the language teaching scene. Figure 2.1 provides an updated visual representation or "map" of the currently most well-known variants of CBI.

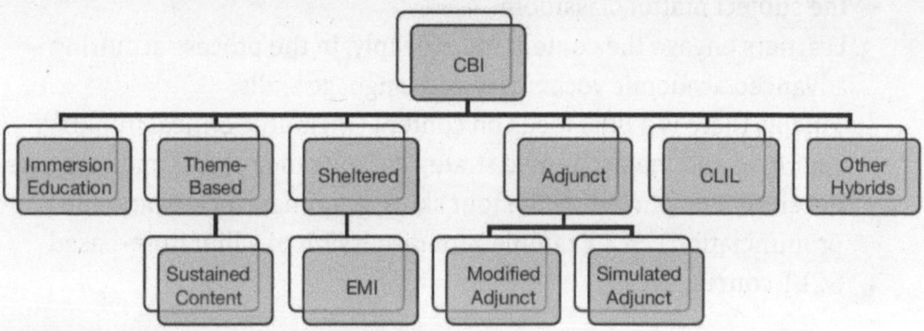

Figure 2.1: An Updated Map of CBI

Newer and Hybrid Models of CBI

Evident in Figure 3 is the fact that the three prototype models of theme-based, sheltered, and adjunct instruction are still very much present on the SFL teaching scene. However, for all three prototypes, there are offshoots of the original models, indicating directions in which CBI has evolved to accommodate specific student populations, teaching settings, and local resources/logistics.

Sustained Content Language Teaching

The first of these approaches, **sustained content language teaching** (SCLT), has been previously briefly mentioned. Sustained content courses are similar to sheltered content courses but are taught by a language instructor rather than a content instructor. According to Murphy and Stoller (2001), the two major components of SCLT include a focus on the exploration of a single content area or carrier topic over the course of a unit, along with a complementary focus on L2 learning and teaching. The authors list these advantages of SCLT over more traditional theme-based instruction:

1. Topics are "stretched" over a whole term or an entire school year—thus avoiding the pitfalls of the theme-based "potpourri" approach (Jacobs, 1989) where content is presented in bits and pieces with no obvious connections in terms of content or language selection.
2. The use of sustained content simulates the conditions and demands of the subject matter classroom.
3. Learners engage the content more deeply, in the process acquiring advanced academic vocabulary and language skills.
4. Finally, there is a dual focus on content (including critical thinking, cognitive and metacognitive strategies, and study skills) and language development (including the four skills, grammar, vocabulary, and pronunciation). See Example 7 for discussion of a literature-based SCLT course.

Example 7: A University-Level Sustained Content Course

Brinton (2001) provides an example of a SCLT elective literature course taught to advanced L2 students at the University of California, Los Angeles. The course, "Focus on the City of Angels," revolves around the single extended theme of the city of Los Angeles. Opting to depart from the traditional format for literature courses in which students read excerpts from great works of literature, Brinton instead organizes the course around the theme of dealing with life and urban issues in Los Angeles. Students read essays, autobiographies, poems, short stories, and a novel; in all of these, the city plays a central role and exerts its unique influence on character and plot. Integral to the course are activities that acquaint students with literary devices (e.g., plot, setting, character development); however, equally important are activities (e.g., guided discussions, response journals, stylistic analysis of word choice) that use the content to enhance students' language and critical-thinking skills and introduce Los Angeles to international students.

Content and Language Integrated Learning

The turn of the century saw the emergence and exponential growth of **content and language integrated learning** (CLIL), particularly in Europe. According to Marsh (2003), CLIL:

> . . . refers to any dual-focused educational context in which an additional language, thus not usually the first language of the learners involved, is used as a medium in the teaching and learning of non-language content. It is dual-focused because whereas attention may be predominantly on either subject-specific content or language, both are always accommodated. (Introduction, para. 1)

CLIL, then, is a dual language model that represents a response to the multilingual needs and goals of global economies through the delivery of certain subject matter courses in the students' L2. With its goal of creating global citizens, CLIL lends itself to settings (e.g., the European Union) where a language other than the students' home language serves as a lingua franca or language of wider communication (Coyle et al., 2010). Since its beginnings, CLIL has spread rapidly throughout Europe and elsewhere worldwide.

CLIL shares key features with other forms of CBI, especially (partial) immersion and sheltered instruction. In both of these approaches, students study subject matter delivered in a language other than that of their L1; L2 acquisition occurs as a "by-product" of the rich exposure to meaningful language in the subject matter classroom. Additionally, in both approaches, language and content aims are integrated and the instructor's task is to both make content comprehensible to the targeted student population and to support language acquisition. So-called "hard" CLIL is a form of subject teaching in the L2 that emphasizes academic achievement in the subject matter and treats language development as a kind of "bonus." "Soft" CLIL, on the other hand, may be offered for a shorter period (e.g., half a year) and places emphasis on both subject matter achievement and language development

(Ball et al., 2015). This form of CLIL is most similar to sustained content or theme-based curricula in ESL/EFL classes.

However, there are important differences between CLIL and CBI as well. For one, CLIL is largely driven by a language policy that embraces the development of multilingual/multicultural individuals who can function in today's global society. Students' exposure to L2 subject matter instruction is systematically "phased in" over time, with the number of hours of L2 content instruction increasing with grade level. Sheltered instruction, on the other hand, is typically driven by pressing educational needs in settings where large numbers of school-age children speak home languages other than the language of school and may enter the school system at any time during the academic year. The end goal of sheltered instruction is to transition students from the sheltered to the mainstream classroom. Most English learners in the U.S.-sheltered programs have very different sociolinguistic profiles than CLIL students; they typically come from immigrant families and are adjusting to life in their new country. CLIL, in contrast, is often seen as an elite programmatic option with "high social value for parents" (Ball et al., 2015, p. 11).

Although some schools of thought differentiate CLIL from immersion education and CBI in general (see, for example, Coyle et al., 2010), today the consensus is that CLIL and CBI share more commonalities than differences and that they belong to the same tradition (Brinton & Snow, 2017; Cañado, 2016; Dalton-Puffer et al., 2014; Dalton-Puffer, 2017). Example 8 provides details on soft versus hard CLIL.

Example 8: Soft vs. Hard CLIL

Soft CLIL: Twelve-year-olds studying English in a pilot program in Italy, the Netherlands, and Spain are introduced to conceptual content through extended project work on inventions (drawn from the field of technology). Subthemes of the two-month unit, taught by English-language instructors, include "Inventions through time," "Inventors and their inventions," and "The process of inventing" (Ball et al., 2015). Throughout the unit, the teachers focus on language issues, which are outlined for them in the teachers' guide.

Hard CLIL: L1 Spanish-speaking students aged 14–15 are enrolled in secondary school in an urban area of Madrid taking a CLIL geography course taught through the medium of English. The teacher, also an L1 Spanish speaker, is a content specialist in geography and history with several years of experience teaching these subjects using CLIL. The students are working on a project involving urban land use and have proposed building a skateboard park in a plot of unused land. (Dalton-Puffer, 2017)

English-Medium Instruction

Often referred to as the tertiary education variant of CLIL, **English-medium instruction** (EMI) refers to content instruction delivered in the students' L2. Central to the appeal of EMI are the dual aims of creating multilingual citizens and internationalizing tertiary institutions—that is, to appeal to international students for whom EMI courses are an enrollment incentive and thus a financial boon to the institution (Doiz et al., 2013). EMI course offerings have multiplied dramatically in recent years, not only in Europe but as well in many other parts of the globe, with more than 60 percent of all postgraduate courses in Europe currently being offered through EMI (Macaro, 2015).

That being said, the broad implementation of EMI—particularly in European countries such as Sweden, Slovenia, and Iceland ("CLIL debate," 2005)—has come under some scrutiny, with critics claiming that English is given unequal power vis-à-vis the L1. According to the Conseil Européen pour les Langues/European Language Council (2016), the decision in the European Union to use English as the lingua franca of academia may be to the "detriment of multilingualism and linguistic diversity" (p. 3).

The implementation of EMI differs widely from country to country, as well as from institution to institution. In particular, this variation pertains to the degree to which language support or an intentional focus on language skills is present. In what might be termed the "weak" version of EMI, L2 students are exposed to content delivered in English with little or no attention paid to language skills (Dueñas, 2003). On the other end of the spectrum, Brinton (2007) describes "language-enhanced" (also known as "language-sensitive") English-medium courses in which the content and language goals are intentionally aligned and where there is an explicit focus on developing language skills as well as increasing content knowledge.

Whatever model approach is selected, those who implement EMI are bound to encounter many of the same challenges that surface in other forms of integrated language and content learning. These include (1) the requisite threshold level of L2 proficiency needed for both students and faculty to participate successfully in and benefit from EMI; (2) effective means of assessing this proficiency; (3) faculty familiarity with and buy-in to the EMI model, and (4) training of faculty to assist them in delivering content effectively to L2 students along with providing language support if part of program objectives. For more details see the "Issues in implementation" section. Example 9 provides information on an EMI course at the graduate level.

Example 9: An EMI Course for Graduate Students in Denmark

Kling (2017) reports on an EMI course for Masters of Science students at the University of Copenhagen. The course, Drug Discovery and Development, is taught by an L2 speaker of English and enrolls students from a broad spectrum of national, language, and disciplinary backgrounds. Its aim is to introduce students to the various phases of drug discovery and development. Class sessions provide a venue for students to discuss topics of special interest and establish an opportunity for them to improve their ability to communicate in English. Course assignments include literature searches and report writing. The end goal is that students will be able to display an understanding of and the ability to use technical terms related to drug discovery and development learned over the term.

Modified and Simulated Adjunct Models

In the prototype model of adjunct instruction, the instructors of two separate classes (a content and a language class) coordinate their instructional aims, with the content class driving curricular decisions and the language class narrowing in on the language skills that students need to function in the content course. Numerous modifications have been made to this model to make it more responsive to setting variables. Iancu (2002), for example, describes an adaptation of the adjunct model to the intensive English-language program (IEP) setting—in this case, an introductory-level university content course was adjuncted to four separate skill-based IEP courses (listening and note-taking, reading, academic writing, and speech). This modification allowed the model to be used with students at a lower level of English-language proficiency and was therefore well suited to the IEP setting. Snow and Kamhi-Stein

(2002) describe another modification at the university level in which general education content courses were paired instead with a study group, co-taught by a language specialist and a peer study group leader (i.e., an undergraduate student who had successfully completed the content course). In this version of the adjunct model, extensive faculty development took place with faculty of the targeted general education courses redesigning their courses to make the content more accessible to language minority students and to teach the language skills needed to meet the demands of the content assignments (Snow, 1997; Srole, 1997). Example 10 provides details on a simulated adjunct model taught at the university level.

Example 10: A Simulated Adjunct Model at the University Level

Brinton and Jensen (2002) describe a "simulated adjunct model" (p. 125) in which video excerpts of university content lectures and their accompanying course readings from authentic sources form the core of sustained content units in the university's EAP program. Selected from a cross-curricular sampling of general education courses (such as Introduction to Sociology, Communication Studies, and Atmospheric Sciences), the units also contain materials for language and academic skills development along with other theme-related enrichment activities (e.g., political cartoons, newspaper articles, short-story excerpts) that complement the content of each unit (see also Brinton et al., 1997).

Other Hybrid Models

One difficulty of describing other hybrid models is that many variants or "twists" of the CBI model that have arisen in response to local contexts and student needs are neither widely reported nor captured in print. One notable exception, however, are writing intensive (WI) courses. Such courses, which are offered in various discipline areas across the curriculum, typically have these characteristics (Townsend, 2001):

- The student-to-instructor ratio is small, ensuring more individual attention to student writing.

- Courses are taught by senior content area faculty members who have attended writing across the curriculum workshops.
- A specified number of writing assignments are required for the course to qualify as WI.
- Writing assignments require multiple drafts, span a variety of genres, and constitute a specified percentage of students' final grade in the content course.

Example 11 provides information on a WI course for university undergraduate students.

Example 11: A WI Course for University Undergraduate Students

Jensen reports on a WI course designed for multilingual writers and offered through the Department of Applied Linguistics at the University of California, Los Angeles (L. Jensen, personal communication, 2010). In the course—An Introduction to Language Learning and Language Teaching—students complete four multidraft written assignments: (1) a personal reflection on their L2 learning experiences; (2) an analysis of observations conducted in second language classrooms; (3) a review of a recent ESL or EFL language textbook, written to publication specifications, and (4) a research paper examining a popular conception of language learning that drew on a minimum of three sources. In addition to these formal writing assignments, the students also post and respond to weekly reading reaction journals on the course management site.

Adaptation of the Model to Innovative Contexts

Three final examples attest to the flexible and ever-evolving nature of CBI (Brinton & Snow, 2017) as program designers apply it in new, as yet untested, contexts. The first of these innovative applications is reported by McCloskey (2017), who adapted thematic instruction to a summer camp program for middle school students from diverse countries and cultures. The program, Teaching Tolerance through English, took place near Lake Ballaton in

Hungary and had as its goal to foster cross-cultural acceptance and conflict resolution in a region that was still healing from ethnic wars and where discrimination against Roma communities continued to be an issue. McCloskey outlines four main goals of the program: (1) to develop an ongoing community of teachers and learners to extend the tolerance-building efforts beyond the confines of the camp experience; (2) to promote the concept of peaceful coexistence, including respect for other cultures and for human/civil rights; (3) to introduce interactive teaching techniques (e.g., cooperative learning, readers' theater, jigsaw activities) and language development strategies (e.g., quickwrite, language frames, and word squares), and (4) to increase participants' overall English language proficiency through the two-week summer camp immersion experience.

A second innovative application of CBI is reported by Chou and Lee (2017), who adapted a CBI approach in the ESP context of a private college specializing in art and architecture. The college, located in San Francisco, California, enrolls a high percentage of international students requiring language support and offers an onsite, as well as a fully online, program. In both cases, the authors contend that CBI as an approach provides instructors with the necessary flexibility to tailor it to the demands of the various courses offered at the college while at the same time providing students with the necessary language scaffolding for them to participate successfully in their content area classes.

A final example of innovative CBI programming is reported by van Wyk (2017), who designed a "hybrid adjunct model" (p. 183) course for first-year students from diverse linguistic backgrounds (e.g., Sesotho, Setswana, isiXhosa, and Afrikaans) at the University of the Free State in Bloemfontein, South Africa. Adding to the challenge of teaching such diverse linguistic groups, the university also faces the situation that the majority of the students admitted to the first-year program come from under-resourced schools and enter the university lacking essential academic literacy skills. To address the resulting very high attrition rate among its first-year students, the university designed a special hybrid adjunct model course in which students enroll in two courses—a content area class and a non-credit-bearing language tutorial class. However, unlike the typical adjunct model course, those teaching the language tutorial classes are not trained language instructors but rather receive ongoing curricular and pedagogical guidance from a designated language specialist. As van Wyk (2017) reports, the CBI approach employed allows the university the means to provide cross-curricular support specifically tailored to the content-area needs of the students.

Reflection

1. Despite many new models of CBI, the three original "prototype" models of theme-based, sheltered, and adjunct still endure. Why do you believe this is the case?
2. Looking at the updated map of CBI in Figure 2.1, which model do you believe would best fit your teaching context?
3. Do you believe the authors are justified in classifying all of the new models in the map as CBI? Why/why not?
4. Which factors do you believe led course developers to create newer, hybrid models of CBI?

3. A Rationale and Support From Research

Although early CBI works focused more on defining the approach itself and discussing aspects of its implementation, much has been written in the years since the approach first appeared on the SFL teaching scene to provide a grounded rationale for CBI and to argue its merits through support derived from empirical research.

A Rationale for CBI

A clear and compelling rationale for CBI is provided by Genesee and Lindholm-Leary (2013), who note the following arguments for its efficacy:

1. It allows L2 learners to develop their language skills in tandem with social and cognitive skills.
2. Its focus on providing meaningful and relevant academic content and creating opportunities for purposeful communication motivates L2 learning.
3. Exposure to content enables learners to map new language onto meaning and thought.
4. CBI provides exposure to structural and functional language variation in different contexts of use, thus enabling L2 learners to acquire forms and functions that are authentic and useful.
5. It facilitates opportunities for learners to link what is new to already known ideas and skills, thus providing opportunities for deeper processing and learning

Some additional benefits include the fact that CBI provides a meaningful context for the language items being presented and serves as an organizing principle for decisions about the selection and sequencing of language items. It also provides rich opportunities for L2 acquisition to occur by providing the input that learners need, creating opportunities for negotiation of meaning about meaningful content, and pushing students to develop appropriate and accurate output. Finally, it exposes students to high-level academic content and encompasses work on academic skills that can transfer to other academic disciplines (Snow, 2014).

Support From Research

Arguments supporting a CBI approach can be both of a direct and an indirect nature. Direct support can be found in empirical research conducted in the fields of second language acquisition (SLA) and cognitive/educational psychology, while indirect support can be drawn from well-known CBI frameworks and from the reported outcomes of CBI programs in a variety of instructional settings. Fitzsimmons-Doolan and colleagues (2017) summarize several sources of support for CBI, elucidating some of the more significant findings.

Support From SLA Research and Related Fields

SLA research has long stressed the importance of both linguistic *input* (the language that learners are exposed to) and linguistic *output* (the language produced by learners) in L2 acquisition. A clear strength of CBI according to SLA theories is its emphasis on input (in the form of challenging thematic or disciplinary texts that learners are exposed to) and output (in the form of the topic-related productive and/or form-focused activities, both spoken and written) that learners engage in (Ellis, 2008; Lyster, 2007). Acquisition is further fostered through the resulting *negotiation of meaning* that learners engage in as they perform tasks related to the CBI unit's content (Dalton-Puffer, 2011).

Additional research support for CBI comes from the field of cognitive psychology, specifically from studies looking at the role played by motivation in L2 acquisition. Studies in immersion education have long shown a direct correlation between these two entities (cf. Gardner et al., 1997). More recent work in motivation underscores this correlation, stressing the complex, dynamic interplay between motivation and language use (Dörnyei et al., 2015). Lightbown (2014) postulates that the intensive nature of CBI classes (in contrast to more traditional FL classes) allows students to more consciously observe their linguistic progress, thus strengthening their language-learning motivation. This observation is borne out in several studies of CBI programs (Doiz et al., 2014; Wu & Chang, 2010).

Research into the acquisition of academic literacy also sheds light on how a CBI approach can support L2 students' acquisition of academic language and the genre-specific features of different content areas. Accordingly, theories such as Cummins' (2000) distinction between **basic interpersonal communication skills** (BICS, or the language of interpersonal communication) and **cognitive academic language proficiency** (CALP, or the language and skills needed for academic achievement) support a CBI approach, which provides learners with intensive exposure to challenging academic texts and assists them with strategies for successfully completing the accompanying academic tasks—thus fostering their acquisition of CALP.

As for support from cognitive and educational psychology, Fitzsimmons-Doolan and colleagues (2017) note that these fields provide some of the most persuasive support for CBI. Regarding cognitive theories of learning, for example, research into **implicit learning** (the acquisition of new knowledge without the awareness of that acquisition) and **learning automaticity** (unintentional, stimulus-driven learning) both lend support for CBI, where the learning trajectory typically follows a research-supported sequence that begins with explicit, cognitive learning, transitions to implicit, associative learning reinforced through practice and systematic exposure to content, and concludes with autonomous learning that helps to develop automaticity (Grabe, 2009). Further, Fitzsimmons-Doolan and colleagues (2017) note that through its coherent presentation of themes, texts, topics, threads, tasks, and transitions (see Stoller & Grabe, 2017), CBI provides the ideal circumstances for depth of processing to occur, hence leading to better student recall. Finally, Fitzsimmons-Doolan and colleagues (2017) note that an additional strength of CBI is its use of techniques to help students recognize discourse structures—for example, having students analyze a text with reference to its discourse markers (e.g., signal words or transitional expressions), or asking them to "map" the organization of a text (e.g., creating a graphic organizer to show cause and effect). Such techniques follow the recommendations of discourse comprehension-processing research (Grabe, 2009).

Further insights from cognitive psychology also underscore the critical role played by motivation (as previously noted in the research on SLA) and expertise. According to research in this field, motivation and interest are both nurtured through activities that involve challenging information and require complex skills—both important goals in the CBI classroom. According to Grabe (2009), as task complexity in CBI activities builds, so too do the opportunities for students to engage in flow, i.e., situations in which students' personal skills match the challenge presented by a given task. This in turn increases students' intrinsic motivation to learn both content and language in the CBI classroom. Finally, regarding findings on expertise building, CBI falls in line with research that recommends opportunities for repeated practice of language skills and strategy training within a specific content area. This condition most definitely holds true for sustained content instruction in CBI, where strategy training and abundant language practice are contextualized via a specific theme or content domain.

Support From CBI Program Outcomes

According to Fitzsimmons-Doolan and colleagues (2017), an important source of support for CBI comes from the various instructional frameworks designed to guide CBI practitioners and ensure the successful outcomes of CBI practice. These frameworks include the SIOP (Echevarría et al., 2017), the Cognitive Academic Language Learning Approach (CALLA) (Chamot, 2009), Concept-Oriented Reading Instruction (CORI) (Guthrie et al., 2007), and CLIL (Doiz et al., 2013). These frameworks all developed independently; they also vary in the settings and student populations they are intended for, and in how CBI practice is conceptualized in each framework. Nonetheless, given the numerous published studies associated with the frameworks, they all contribute significantly to creating a research base that serves to further document successful CBI classroom practices. Among some of the many positive outcomes from the associated research studies that Fitzsimmons-Doolan and colleagues (2017) review are: (a) significant improvement in students' writing abilities and oral proficiency; (b) greater and better exposure to the target language; (c) documented growth of lexical items; (d) gains on content achievement measures and in content knowledge acquisition; (e) positive outcomes for reading comprehension on standardized tests, and (f) enhanced reading-strategy use.

In terms of other reported outcomes from CBI programs, the research base is broadly dispersed in both K–12 and post-secondary contexts and has been carried out in both SFL instructional contexts. Dominating this area of research are the numerous studies related to the immersion context, dating to the early studies of the St. Lambert program (Lambert & Tucker, 1972). Among some of the interesting research findings on immersion students' achievement as summarized by Fitzsimmons-Doolan and colleagues (2017) are equal performance on content mastery as L1 students and higher scores on FL achievement measures in all areas of language skills than students taking a traditional FL class. Other interesting outcomes reported in the FL setting are higher scores in both language and content on university gatekeeping exams, along with higher than average acceptance into colleges and universities by those graduating from immersion programs. Finally, studies (see, for example, Song, 2006) report that students who participated in an integrated language and content course at the outcome of their tertiary education demonstrated greater retention, higher grade point averages, and higher graduation rates than a matched cohort that did not experience the content-linked class.

Reflection

1. Consider the rationale presented for CBI. Which argument(s) do you find the most compelling? Why?
2. Fitzsimmons-Doolan and colleagues (2017) distinguish between direct and indirect support for CBI. What do they mean by this distinction?
3. Are you familiar with any of the instructional frameworks mentioned as providing support for CBI? If so, which?
4. In your opinion, which of the areas of research (SLA research or research in cognitive/educational psychology) provides the most compelling support for CBI? Why? Can you think of any other areas of research (such as research in motivation)?

4. Issues In Implementation

As Brinton and colleagues (2003) note, there are numerous issues that impact the successful implementation of CBI. These include but are not limited to: administrative issues (e.g., where the impetus for implementing CBI comes from and who carries responsibility for the program's implementation); program design issues (e.g., whether the primary objective is to teach language or to teach content, or both, and how far-reaching the planned changes are); student issues (e.g., students' L2 proficiency level, their prior educational background, and their needs and interests); staffing issues (e.g., whether instructors have the necessary language proficiency and background in CBI and whether they are willing to take on new roles in their teaching); assessment issues (e.g., the relative degree to which content and language should be weighted in the assessment scheme), and finally, program evaluation issues (e.g., student achievement, teacher and student attitudes, and the quality of the curriculum and materials).

Primary Issues Impacting Successful Implementation

According to research studies in CBI, however, there appear to be three primary issues that are mentioned repeatedly as impacting the implementation of CBI. These include: (1) the lack of attention to form in CBI; (2) the balance of attention to language vis-à-vis content, and (3) the power imbalance between language and content instructors.

Lack of Attention to Form

With respect to the first of these issues, Eskey (1997) notes that CBI tends to "come down hard" (p. 139) on the side of fluency, thus often paying inadequate attention to form. This is echoed by research conducted by Brinton and Holten (2001), who note that language instructors often spend more classroom time reviewing content than focusing on language. They term this phenomenon "content envy." Lyster (2007), in his research in language and content integrated classrooms, documents similar findings—that is, the focus on language is often incidental. As a possible solution to this shortcoming, he suggests that course designers proactively plan for the following sequence of language-focused activities: (a) a **noticing phase**, where a specific language feature or features are made more salient in a text; (b) an **awareness phase**, where students can reflect on and manipulate the language feature; (c) a **guided practice phase**, where students are pushed to use the new language feature in controlled contexts and receive feedback on their production, and (d) an **autonomous practice phase**, where students use the new language feature to discuss or recapitulate disciplinary or thematic concepts in a more communicative context (Lyster, 2017). And, finally, Valeo (2013) in a controlled classroom-based study of an occupation-specific language program for adults notes that a focus-on-form approach results in significant gains in language as well as in content mastery.

Balance of Attention to Language vis-à-vis Content

Next, as pertains to achieving a balance of language and content in the integrated classroom, research yields these findings: Davison (2005) in a study of "subject English" as a content course notes that the definition of what is language and what is content can shift according to the disciplinary community—that is, the very notions of language and content are subject to interpretation. Creese (2005), in her study of collaborating teachers in U.K. secondary school classrooms, concludes that language work in the content classroom is typically given low status. Tan (2011), in her study of math, science, and language teachers in the Malaysian context, documents that teachers' beliefs about their role as "only content teachers or only language teachers" (p. 325) limited the effectiveness of CBI. Cammarata and Tedick (2012), examining the practices of three immersion teachers, conclude that the teachers should engage in "pedagogical awakening" as they struggle to balance language and content. And, finally, Snow and colleagues (2017) describe different conceptualizations of academic language features and provide specific examples of classroom activities at elementary, secondary, and post-secondary levels of how teachers can teach students the language needed for content mastery.

Baecher and colleagues (2017) agree that teachers in the language and content integrated classroom—especially teachers in training and novice teachers—often struggle with how to integrate a focus on language in the lessons they deliver. As a result, language goals are often sacrificed for content goals—this despite widespread recognition of the need to integrate an intentional focus on language in the CBI classroom and despite state-mandated standards that typically govern this practice. To address the issue, the authors suggest that teachers need to be trained (at the pre- or in-service level) to plan and design language- and content-focused lessons via specific instruction in lesson planning. They propose that this take place at the unit rather than lesson level, with content being foregrounded in some of the unit's lessons while language is foregrounded in others. Concerning the latter, they note that language performance tasks need to be planned around relevant language functions (e.g., the notion of persuasion, which entails the use of modals, parallel structure, and rhetorical questions) and that tasks need to take into consideration the language that students need in order to discuss the unit's content. Finally, the authors note that when implementing the lesson, teachers need to be aware that while much of the language instruction that is delivered can be pre-planned, some of it will be incidental (i.e., responding to language issues that arise as the instruction is being delivered).

Power Imbalance

A final area that impacts the successful implementation of CBI models is the perennial issue in CBI of power relations between content and language teachers. A classic in its own right, Goldstein and colleagues' (1997) research highlights the subservient position that many language instructors take to content instructors in adjunct contexts. Accordingly, the authors dubbed the phenomenon they observed "the flight attendant syndrome." Goldstein (2017), in an updated look at the issue, notes that while the adjunct model is predicated on a mutually beneficial working relationship between the content and language instructors, the majority of adjunct language instructors in her study still report working without adequate compensation, lacking opportunities to coordinate with their respective content counterpart, and being disrespected both by administrators and content faculty. Arkoudis' (2005) research applies insights from appraisal and positioning theory to examine teacher power relationships in planning sessions. These relationships are shown to negatively impact teachers' efforts to balance language and content in their courses. Similarly, Tan (2011) reports that overall, the mathematics and science instructors in her study tended to dismiss the importance of language instruction for the conceptual learning of their students. In their research, Pawan and Ortloff (2011) note tensions between language and content faculty.

They conclude with a call to faculty from both disciplines for interprofessionality. This call is further echoed by Pawan and Greene (2017), who suggest that applying frameworks of trust and collaboration can ameliorate the power relationship between content and language faculty.

Issues In Curriculum Design and Assessment

Before concluding the discussion of implementation issues, a few thoughts regarding curriculum design and assessment are in order. The case can be made that the issues involved in designing curriculum or assessing student performance is not significantly different in CBI than in any other form of language syllabus. Careful attention must be paid in curriculum design to articulate any guiding principles that undergird the curriculum; contextual factors (e.g., socioeconomic, political) must be taken into consideration; learners' needs and interests must be assessed and program goals formulated accordingly; course content must be selected to match these needs and interests; items in the curriculum must be organized and sequenced; and an assessment plan must be formulated that is in accord with all of the above (Graves, 2014). Further, when fine-tuning the assessment plan, students' proficiency level must be identified, the formative and summative purposes of assessment must be considered, and appropriate language assessment tools must be selected and linked to learning goals, etc. (Katz, 2014).

However, as Nunan (2017) reminds us, CBI is an integrated approach and, as such, content specification and course outcomes must be identified in tandem. Further, he notes, the relative roles of content, tasks, and projects within the curriculum must be identified and a determination made as to which of these will drive the curriculum. Especially as it pertains to the theme-based model of CBI, there are often issues of coherence that need to be considered. So while strengths of the theme-based curriculum are that themes can connect learners to the real world, expose them to authentic issues, and provide a carrier topic for the teaching of skills and language forms and functions, there are potential pitfalls as well. These include the fact that certain themes that are selected may lack novelty and/or cultural relevance, and as a result may not be of high interest to students. And perhaps even more importantly, the CBI course may lack coherence from unit to unit, as students move from the study of "bugs" to "extreme weather," to "cool vacations," without a clear understanding of why. This potential pitfall, often referred to as "the potpourri approach to theme selection," is particularly common in textbook treatments of theme-based instruction, where units tend to move from topic to topic without any clear signaling of how the various topics are interrelated. To lend coherence to the theme-based curriculum, Stoller and Grabe (2017) suggest a 6Ts model of curriculum design. In this model, a central idea or **theme** is first identified to complement student interests and analyzed for its subunits or **topics** that expand the curriculum. Following identification of these first two Ts, theme-related **texts** are selected and **tasks** are formulated to assist students in processing both the content and language being presented. The final two Ts consist of **transitions** (which provide links from topic to topic, from task to task, or from text to text) and **threads** (which provide links from theme to theme in a multi-themed curriculum).

Implementing CBI also involves familiarity with the model and its underlying principles along with buy-in by key faculty. This is especially true in the EFL context, where existing teaching philosophies may be at odds with CBI pedagogies (Harada, 2017). Also to be considered is how the CBI curriculum fits with state- or nationally mandated standards. To achieve the fit, Reynolds (2017) suggests employing a backward curriculum design process, beginning with the standards and final assessments first, in order to inform the development of the CBI unit. In this manner, language skills and content can be identified and balanced, and texts can be analyzed to determine the extent to which the language being presented is in accordance with the standards. This analysis in turn can assist the course developer in determining the academic and linguistic objectives of the unit.

Finally, as pointed out by Andrade and Green (2017), the major conundrum in CBI assessment lies in the fact that it is difficult (if not impossible) to separate language and content. From the assessment perspective, this means that traditional language assessment procedures (where test measures are stripped of content to the extent possible so as not to advantage a given learner) are not feasible. In this manner, the what, why, and how of language assessment take on different dimensions in CBI than they do in other types of language curricula. To address the complexity of assessing students in CBI, Andrade and Green suggest these five guidelines:

1. Establish clear outcomes for both language and content.
2. Create test tasks that reflect those that are typical in the content domain.
3. Determine both formative and summative measures of the academic tasks students need to successfully navigate the content.

4. Evaluate the various assessment procedures vis-à-vis student performance and, where necessary, rethink these procedures to better meet student needs.
5. Be prepared to justify how assessment decisions reflect the stated student achievement objectives.

Reflection

1. Numerous issues that may impede the success of CBI have been listed. Do you believe these issues are specific to CBI, or are they more general issues encountered in the design and implementation of SFL courses? Explain.
2. Which of the three central issues impacting the success of CBI do you see as a bigger priority—attention to form, achieving a balance of language and content, or the collaboration of language and content faculty. Why?
3. In your opinion, which factors regarding designing a CBI curriculum are the most challenging? Explain.
4. Explain what is meant by a "potpourri approach." How can the 6Ts framework help lend coherence?
5. According to Andrade and Green, what makes language assessment in CBI different from traditional language assessment?

5. A Research Agenda for CBI

CBI theory and practice have advanced considerably since the approach first appeared on the language teaching scene back in the late 1970s. Not only has CBI expanded its influence around the globe, but the various models of CBI have morphed and developed in ways that allow it to better serve a wide variety of learning populations and settings. This same claim of growth and development also applies to the types of research conducted in the field, which has expanded vastly over the intervening decades. Zappa-Hollman and Duff (2017) respond to this growth by charting an ambitious research agenda for CBI in the future. This agenda includes:

- diversifying CBI research to include a greater range of geographical, linguistic, and educational contexts
- broadening the disciplines examined from their current humanities and social science base to include more science and applied science contexts
- including an examination of the role played in CBI classrooms by the L1 and by translanguaging practices (the classroom utilization of the languages of multilingual speakers for meaning making)
- expanding research on CBI teacher education (both pre-service and in-service)
- achieving a better balance in CBI research between differing research paradigms such as quantitative vs. qualitative research, action research, multimodal research (research examining alternate modes of instructional delivery such as non-verbal or visual), and finally critical research (research examining CBI practices from a global, perspective such as the potential of EMI to dominate the global scene and diminish the role of local languages in higher education).

According to Zappa-Hollman and Duff, expanding CBI's research agenda in the above-noted ways can help, among other things, to more accurately: (1) identify and measure CBI program outcomes; (2) analyze sociocultural practices (such as participation and student agency); (3) document growth in learners' linguistic and/or academic abilities; and (4) influence critical decisions regarding program design and implementation along with program-related research. This expansion of the research agenda should also help to identify new opportunities for students who have not typically participated in CBI programs and critically assess the extent to which given program design features may advantage learners from more privileged socioeconomic backgrounds.

Reflection

1. Zappa-Hollman and Duff (2017) see a need for diversifying CBI research to include a greater range of geographical, linguistic, and educational contexts. Which factors do you believe lie behind the domination of Western contexts regarding research on CBI? How might this domination be overcome?
2. Why might it be important to expand the research domain of CBI to include more science and applied science contexts? Do you agree that this is a priority?
3. Zappa-Hollman and Duff (2017) also suggest expanding the research on teacher education. Name three issues that you believe should be researched regarding CBI teacher education. Why do you believe these are important?
4. Which of the research paradigms (qualitative vs. quantitative, action research, multimodal research, and critical research) are you familiar with? Which type of research is most meaningful to you in your current position? How can different research paradigms answer different research questions in CBI?

6. Conclusions

At this point, it is appropriate to ponder the future of CBI. After all, the movement is close to 40 years old and appears to be a still vibrant force in the field of SFL teaching. Snow (2014) ventures the following thoughts on the issue:

> The teaching of language through content is not so much a method as a reorientation to what is meant by *content* in language teaching. The literature offers strong theoretical support for content-based approaches and abundant examples of successful programs in SFL settings . . . As [it] enters its fifth decade, we share Wesche's (2010) positive outlook that CBLT: ". . . is likely to continue to flourish, particularly in contexts where learners' main opportunity for developing advanced L2 proficiency is a school or post-secondary context and where they need to develop academic L2 ability." (p. 452)

As we have discussed, there remain a number of challenges that are pervasive in CBI. These include (among others) the collaboration of content and language faculty, the willingness and ability of content faculty to assume responsibility for language instruction, effective means of sheltering content delivery for L2 learners, the threshold level of proficiency needed for learners to function in the various models of CBI, and appropriate means of assessing both language and content in an integrated approach. These challenges notwithstanding, we contend that CBI is a highly flexible approach that provides a powerful means of structuring the syllabus for both general purpose and EAP courses.

As an abbreviated version of the full volume, this e-book can touch only briefly on issues discussed in greater depth in the book itself. It should nonetheless be clear to readers that CBI is a vibrant approach to curriculum design that is able to "flex" to fit a wide variety of student populations, settings, and program goals. Those readers wanting a more in-depth treatment of programs mentioned briefly in this e-single or of the full array of programs described in the volume itself are cordially invited to peruse the full volume, which contains in-depth discussions of a wide variety of CBI-related issues as well as descriptions of programs in both the ESL and EFL settings. The volume is divided into six parts: Part I traces the history of CBI, proposes a classification of models and varieties, discusses ongoing challenges, and provides research support for CBI. Part II focuses on programs, curriculum, and lesson designs, featuring chapters on the Six Ts approach, strategic planning, and scaffolding strategies. Part III takes up innovative applications of CBI and includes a variety of models in diverse CBI settings. Part IV establishes connections between CBI and other approaches like ESP, EAP, and corpus linguistics. Part V discusses assessment in CBI, and Part VI explores ongoing challenges. Each of the chapters containing program descriptions begins with a "glimpse" into an actual CBI classroom through a scenario that brings the setting and student population to life. This scenario is followed by a characterization of the CBI model under discussion, a review of the pertinent literature, a discussion of key issues and challenges, and observations/activities and principles that underlie each topic. The chapters conclude with a proposed research agenda related to issues germane to the specific form of CBI under discussion. If your appetite for CBI is whetted, then we invite you to read *The Content-Based Classroom: New Perspectives on Integrating Language and Content* (2017).

7. For Further Reading

Brinton, D. M., Snow, M. A., & Wesche, M. B. (2003). *Content-based second language instruction* (Michigan Classics ed.). Ann Arbor: University of Michigan Press.

The Michigan Classics edition of Brinton and colleagues' 1989 text contains an updated preface along with an epilogue and a glossary of key terms. The remainder of the volume contains the intact content of the original edition: a description of the three "prototype" models of content-based instruction (theme-based, sheltered, and adjunct); treatment of issues pertinent in the successful implementation and assessment of CBI programs, and suggestions for materials development and adaptation.

Crandall, J., & Kaufman, D. (Eds.) (2002). *Content-based instruction in higher education settings*. Alexandria, VA: Teachers of English to Speakers of Other Languages.

In this edited volume, Crandall and Kaufman compile case studies of the application of CBI to higher education settings in both the ESL and EFL settings, written from the point of view of the practitioner. The editors stress the evolving nature of CBI, as reflected in the diverse set of programs described in the volume, all of which have adapted to their immediate context and to the student needs and resources available.

DelliCarpini, M., & Alonso, O. B. (2013). *Content-based instruction*. Alexandria, VA: Teacher of English to Speakers of Other Languages.

This resource book is part of TESOL's English Language Teacher Development series, which aims to provide jargon-free and accessible materials for all types of teachers. It opens with a definition of CBI and presents different models of CBI, delineating features of the models and their advantages and disadvantages. It also contains sections on interdisciplinary teacher collaboration and developing content-driven language and language-driven content objectives.

Each chapter has reflective breaks and activities, making it a suitable text for pre-service and in-service teacher training.

Echevarría, J., Vogt, M. E., & Short, D. J. (2017). *Making content comprehensible for English learners: The SIOP model* (5th ed.). Boston, MA: Pearson.

The fifth edition of this popular text on sheltered instruction focuses on the successful delivery of sheltered content instruction to English learners. With an emphasis on the primary and secondary school contexts, especially with respect to North America, the volume presents recent research that supports the approach along with a description of best practices in the field. The e-text version contains embedded videos and a host of internet resources related to chapter content.

Eskey, D. E. (1997). Syllabus design in content-based instruction. (1997). In M. A. Snow & D. M. Brinton (Eds.), *The content-based classroom: Perspectives on integrating language and content* (pp. 132–141). White Plains, NY: Longman.

In this chapter, Eskey argues that content (in concert with structure and function) provides the missing third dimension in syllabus design for L2 courses. While noting the superiority of the CBI syllabus over other syllabus types (such as the grammatical or notional syllabus), he argues that the CBI syllabus demonstrates certain limitations common to other forms of communicative language teaching, such as a perceived difficulty relating language form to language function and content. He calls for more theoretical work into the relation between these aspects of language, and concludes with a discussion of the prospects of developing the CBI syllabus.

Kaufman, D., & Crandall, J. (Eds.) (2005). *Content-based instruction in primary and secondary school settings*. Alexandria, VA: Teachers of English to Speakers of Other Languages.

This companion to Crandall and Kaufman's (2002) edited volume on content-based instruction in higher education focuses on the application of CBI to primary and secondary settings. The volume is divided into three sections, which examine partnerships and constructivist notions in CBI, reflection and inquiry in CBI professional development, and the relation of standards and curriculum assessment to CBI. The volume presents a rich spectrum of CBI paradigms representing the diversity of elementary and secondary-level CBI programs and collaborative partnerships that have emerged in recent years.

Lightbown, P. M. (2014). *Focus on content-based language teaching.* Oxford, England: Oxford University Press.

This well-researched volume presents a wide scope of CBI programs for both language majority and language minority students. Grounding her observations in classroom-based research, the author clearly presents the challenges that instructors face in the CBI classroom and suggests strategies to help them overcome these challenges. Additional online discussion questions and supplementary activities are available.

Mohan, B. (1986). *Language and content.* Reading, MA: Addison-Wesley.

The first volume to treat the integration of language and content, Mohan's 1986 text remains a classic. The bulk of the volume discusses Mohan's knowledge framework, exemplified with sample language and action situations. Of particular interest to today's ongoing discussions of language and content is the final chapter, "Where Language and Content Should Not Be Confused."

Nordmeyer, J., & Barduhn, S. (Eds.) (2010). *Integrating language and content.* Alexandria, VA: Teachers of English to Speakers of Other Languages.

This edited volume from the TESOL Classroom Practice Series showcases 16 contemporary CBI classroom vignettes from around the world. Divided into four subsections, the volume explores how teachers design CBI courses, how they integrate language and content, the evaluation measures used, and ways in which language and content instructors can collaborate. In their introduction to the volume, the editors present key terminology and discuss the intersection of language and content.

REFERENCES

A language for life: Report of the committee of inquiry appointed by the secretary of state for education and science under the chairmanship of Sir Alan Bullock F. B. A. (1975). London, England: Her Majesty's Stationery Office.

Andrade, M. S., & Green, B. A. (2017). Fundamental principles in content-based assessment. In M. A. Snow & D. M. Brinton (Eds.), *The content-based classroom: New perspectives on integrating language and content* (2nd ed., pp. 297–308). Ann Arbor: University of Michigan Press.

Arkoudis, S. (2005). Fusing pedagogic horizons: Language and content teaching in the mainstream. *Linguistics and Education, 16*, 173–187.

Baecher, L., Ediger, A., & Farnsworth, T. (2017). Teacher planning in content-based instruction: Supports for developing novice teachers' language awareness. In M. A. Snow & D. M. Brinton (Eds.), *The content-based classroom: New perspectives on integrating language and content* (2nd ed., pp. 79–96). Ann Arbor: University of Michigan Press.

Ball, P., Kelly, K., & Clegg, J. (2015). *Putting CLIL into practice*. Oxford, England: Oxford University Press.

Bright, A. (2010). Opening the door: Making mathematics accessible to English language learners. In J. Nordmeyer & S. Barduhn (Eds.), *Integrating language and content* (pp. 109–115). Alexandria, VA: Teachers of English to Speakers of Other Languages.

Brinton, D. M. (2001). A theme-based literature course: Focus on the City of Angels. In J. Murphy & P. Byrd, (Eds.), *Understanding the courses we teach: Local perspectives on English language teaching* (pp. 281–308). Ann Arbor: University of Michigan Press.

Brinton, D. M. (2007). Two for one—Language-enhanced content instruction in English for academic purposes. In *Teaching English for specific purposes: Meeting our learners' needs* (pp. 1–16). Alexandria, VA: Teachers of English to Speakers of Other Languages.

Brinton, D. M., Frodesen, J., Holten, C., Jensen, L., & Repath-Martos, L. (1997). *Insights: A content-based ESL text for academic preparation–Books 1 & 2*. White Plains, NY: Addison Wesley Longman.

Brinton, D. M., & Holten, C. (2001). Does the emperor have no clothes? A re-examination of grammar in content-based instruction. In J. Flowerdew, & M. Peacock (Eds.), *Research perspectives on English for academic purposes* (pp. 239–251). Cambridge, England: Cambridge University Press.

Brinton, D. M., & Jensen, L. (2002). Appropriating the adjunct model: English for academic purposes at the university level. In J. Crandall & D. Kaufman (Eds.), *Content-based instruction in higher education settings* (pp. 125–138). Alexandria, VA: Teachers of English to Speakers of Other Languages.

Brinton, D. M., & Snow, M. A. (2017). The evolving architecture of content-based instruction. In M. A. Snow & D. M. Brinton (Eds.), *The content-based classroom: New perspectives on integrating language and content* (2nd ed., pp. 2–20). Ann Arbor: University of Michigan Press.

Brinton, D. M., Snow, M. A., & Wesche, M. B. (1989). *Content-based second language instruction.* New York, NY: Newbury House.

Brinton, D. M., Snow, M. A., & Wesche, M. B. (2003). *Content-based second language instruction* (Michigan Classics ed.). Ann Arbor: University of Michigan Press.

Cammarata, L., & Tedick, D. J. (2012). Balancing content and language in instruction: The experience of immersion teachers. *The Modern Language Journal, 96*(2), 251–269.

Cañado, M. L. P. (2016). From the CLIL craze to the CLIL conundrum: Addressing the current CLIL controversy. *Bellaterra Journal of Teaching and Learning Language and Literature, 9*(1), 9–31. doi:ḫttp://dx.doi.org/10.5565/rev/jtl3.667

Chamot, A. U. (2009). *The CALLA handbook: Implementing the Cognitive Academic Language Learning Approach* (2nd ed.). New York, NY: Pearson.

Chou, L., & Lee, S. (2017). Teaching content and language in art: Onsite and online approaches. In M. A. Snow & D. M. Brinton (Eds.), *The content-based classroom: New perspectives on integrating language and content* (2nd ed., pp. 191–203). Ann Arbor: University of Michigan Press.

CLIL debate questions and answers. (2005, April 20). The Guardian. Retrieved from https://www.theguardian.com/theguardian/2005/apr/20/guardianweekly.guardianweekly13

Conseil Européen pour les Langues / European Language Council. (2016). The role of languages in the European higher education area. *European Journal of Language Policy, 8*(1), 121– 129.

Cory-Wright, K. (2014). *Our World 6.* Boston, MA: National Geographic Learning / Cengage Learning.

Coyle, D., Hood, P., & Marsh, D. (2010). *CLIL: Content and Language Integrated Learning*. Cambridge, England: Cambridge University Press.

Creese, A. (2005). Is this content based language teaching? *Linguistics and Education, 16*, 188– 204.

Cummins, J. (2000). *Language, power, and pedagogy: Bilingual children in the crossfire*. Clevedon, England: Multilingual Matters.

Dalton-Puffer, C. (2011). Content-and-language integrated learning: From practice to principles. *Annual Review of Applied Linguistics, 31*, 182–204.

Dalton-Puffer, C. (2017). Same but different: Content and language integrated learning and content-based instruction. In M. A. Snow & D. M. Brinton (Eds.), *The content-based classroom: New perspectives on integrating language and content* (2nd ed., pp. 151–164). Ann Arbor: University of Michigan Press.

Dalton-Puffer, C., Llinares, A., Lorenzo, F., & Nikula, T. (2014). "*You Can Stand Under My Umbrella*": Immersion, CLIL and Bilingual Education. A Response to Cenoz, Genesee & Gorter. *Applied Linguistics, 35*(2), 213–218.

Davison, C. (2005). Learning your lines: Negotiating language and content in subject English. *Linguistics and Education, 16*, 219–237.

Davison, C., & Williams, A. (2001). Integrating language and content: Unresolved issues. In B. Mohan, C. Leung, & C. Davison (Eds.), *English as a second language in the mainstream: Teaching, learning and identity* (pp. 51–70). Harlow, England: Longman.

Doiz, A., Lasagabaster, D., & Sierra, J. M. (Eds.). (2013). *English-medium instruction at universities: Global challenges.* Bristol, England: Multilingual Matters.

Doiz, A., Lasagabaster, D., & Sierra, J. M. (2014). CLIL and motivation: The effect of individual and contextual variables. *The Language Learning Journal, 42*(2), 209–224.

Dörnyei, Z., MacIntyre, P. D., & Henry, A. (2015). *Motivational dynamics in language learning.* Bristol, England: Multilingual Matters.

Dueñas, M. (2003). A description of prototype models for content-based instruction in higher education. *BELLS: Barcelona English Language and Literature Studies, 12*. Retrieved from http://www.publicacions.ub.edu/revistes/bells12/

Duff, P. A. (2014). Communicative language teaching. In M. Celce-Murcia, D. M. Brinton, & M. A. Snow (Eds.), *Teaching English as a second or foreign language* (4th ed., pp. 15–30). Boston, MA: National Geographic Learning / Heinle Cengage Learning.

Echevarría, J., Vogt, M. E., & Short, D. J. (2017). *Making content comprehensible for English learners: The SIOP model* (5th ed.). Boston, MA: Pearson.

Edwards, H. P., Wesche, M., Krashen, S., Clément, R., & Kruidenier, B. (1984). Second language acquisition through subject matter learning: A study of sheltered psychology classes at the University of Ottawa. *Canadian Modern Language Review, 41*(2), 268–282.

Ellis, R. (2008). *The study of second language acquisition* (2nd ed.). Oxford, England: Oxford University Press.

Eskey, D. E. (1997). Syllabus design in content-based instruction. (1997). In M. A. Snow & D. M. Brinton (Eds.), *The content-based classroom: Perspectives on integrating language and content* (pp. 132–141). White Plains, NY: Longman.

Fitzsimmons-Doolan, S., Grabe, W., & Stoller, F. L. (2017). Research support for content-based instruction. In M. A. Snow & D. M. Brinton (Eds.), *The content-based classroom: New perspectives on integrating language and content* (2nd ed., pp. 21–35). Ann Arbor: University of Michigan Press.

Gardner, R. C., Tremblay, P. F., & Masgoret, A. (1997). Towards a full model of second language learning: An empirical investigation. *Modern Language Journal, 81*(3), 344–362.

Genesee, F. (1987). *Learning through two languages: Studies of immersion and bilingual education*. Rowley, MA: Newbury House.

Genesee, F., & Lindholm-Leary, K. (2013). Two case studies of content-based language education. *Journal of Immersion and Content-Based Language Education, 1*(1), 3–33.

Goldstein, L. M. (2017). Looking back and looking forward at the adjunct model: Are we still smiling through the turbulence? In M. A. Snow & D. M. Brinton (Eds.), *The content-based classroom: New perspectives on integrating language and content* (2nd ed., pp. 338–352). Ann Arbor: University of Michigan Press.

Goldstein, L., Campbell, C., & Clark Cummings, M. (1997). Smiling through the turbulence: The flight attendant syndrome and writing instructor status in the adjunct model. In M. A. Snow, & D. M. Brinton (Eds.), *The content-based classroom: Perspectives on integrating language and content* (pp. 331–339). White Plains, NY: Longman.

Grabe, W. (2009). *Reading in a second language: Moving from theory to practice.* Cambridge, England: Cambridge University Press.

Graves, K. (2014). Syllabus and curriculum design. In M. Celce-Murcia, D. M. Brinton, & M. A. Snow (Eds.), *Teaching English as a second or foreign language* (4th ed., pp. 46–62). Boston, MA: National Geographic Learning / Heinle Cengage Learning.

Guthrie, J. T., McRae, A., & Klauda, S. L. (2007). Contributions of Concept-Oriented Reading Instruction to knowledge for interventions about motivation for reading. *Educational Psychologist, 42*(4), 237–250.

Harada, T. (2017). Developing a content-based English as a foreign language program: Needs analysis and curriculum design at the university level. In M. A. Snow, & D. M. Brinton (Eds.), *The content-based classroom: New perspectives on integrating language and content* (2nd ed., pp. 37–52). White Plains, NY: Longman.

Hauptmann, P. C., Wesche, M. B., & Ready, D. (1988). Second language acquisition through subject matter learning: A follow-up study of sheltered psychology classes at the University of Ottawa. *Language Learning, 38*(3), 439–482.

Hauschild, S., Poltavtchenko, E., & Stoller, F. L. (2012). Going green: Merging environmental education and language instruction. *English Teaching Forum, 2*, 2–13.

Hymes. D. (1971). On communicative competence. Philadelphia: University of Pennsylvania Press.

Iancu, M. (2002). To motivate and educate, collaborate and integrate: The adjunct model in a bridge program. In J. A. Crandall & D. Kaufman (Eds.), *Content-based instruction in higher education settings* (pp. 139–153). Alexandria, VA: Teachers of English to Speakers of Other Languages.

Jacobs, H. H. (1989). (Ed.). The growing need for interdisciplinary content. In *Interdisciplinary curriculum: Design and implementation* (pp. 1–11). Alexandria, VA: Association for Supervision and Curriculum Development.

Katz, A. (2014). Assessment in second language classrooms. In M. Celce-Murcia, D. M. Brinton, & M. A. Snow (Eds.), *Teaching English as a second or foreign language* (4th ed., pp. 320–337). Boston, MA: National Geographic Learning/Heinle Cengage Learning.

Kling, J. (2017). English medium instruction and the international classroom. In M. A. Snow & D. M. Brinton (Eds.), *The content-based classroom: New perspectives on integrating language and content* (2nd ed., pp. 216–227). Ann Arbor: University of Michigan Press.

Krueger, M., & Ryan, F. (Eds.). (1993). Language and content: Discipline- and content-based approaches to language study. Lexington, MA: D. C. Heath and Company.

Lambert, W. E., & Tucker, G. R. (1972). *The bilingual education of children: The St. Lambert Experiment*. Rowley, MA: Newbury House.

Lightbown, P. M. (2014). *Focus on content-based language teaching.* Oxford, England: Oxford University Press.

Lyster, R. (2007). *Learning and teaching languages through content: A counterbalanced approach.* Amsterdam, The Netherlands: John Benjamins.

Lyster, R. (2017). Language-focused instruction in content-based classrooms. In M. A. Snow & D. M. Brinton (Eds.), *The content-based classroom: New perspectives on integrating language and content* (2nd ed., pp. 109–123). Ann Arbor: University of Michigan Press.

Macaro, E. (2015). English medium instruction: Time to start asking some difficult questions. *Modern English Teacher, 24*(2), 4–7.

Marsh, D. (2003, April). The relevance and potential of content and language integrated learning (CLIL) for achieving MT+2 in Europe. ELC Information Bulletin, 9. Retrieved from http://userpage.fu-berlin.de/elc/bulletin/9/en/marsh.html

Met, M. (1999, January). Content-based instruction: Defining terms, making decisions. *NFLC Reports.* Washington, DC: The National Foreign Language Center.

McCloskey, M. L. (2017). From human rights to conflict resolution: Thematic teaching for peace and cross-cultural acceptance. In M. A. Snow & D. M. Brinton (Eds.), *The content-based classroom: New perspectives on integrating language and content* (2nd ed., pp. 138–150). Ann Arbor: University of Michigan Press.

Mohan, B. (1986). *Language and content.* Reading, MA: Addison-Wesley.

Murphy, J. M., & Stoller, F. L. (Eds.). (2001, Summer/Autumn). Sustained-content language teaching: An emerging definition. *TESOL Journal, 10*(2/3), 3–5.

Nunan, D. (2017). The integrated syllabus: Content, tasks, and projects. In M. A. Snow & D. M. Brinton (Eds.), *The content-based classroom: New perspectives on integrating language and content* (2nd ed., pp. 124–136). Ann Arbor: University of Michigan Press.

Parker, R. (1985). The "language across the curriculum" movement: A brief overview and bibliography. *College Composition and Communication, 36*(2), 173–177.

Pawan, F., & Greene, M. C. S. (2017). In trust we collaborate: ESL and content-area teachers working together in content-based language instruction. In M. A. Snow & D. M. Brinton (Eds.), *The content-based classroom: New perspectives on integrating language and content* (2nd ed., pp. 323–337). Ann Arbor: University of Michigan Press.

Pawan, F., & Ortloff, J. H. (2011). Sustaining collaboration: English-as-a-second-language, and content-area teachers. *Teaching and Teacher Education, 27,* 463–471.

Reynolds, K. M. (2015). *Approaches to inclusion English classrooms: A teacher's handbook for content-based instruction.* Bristol, England: Multilingual Matters.

Reynolds, K. M. (2017). Strategic curriculum planning: Standards and objectives in content-based instruction. In M. A. Snow & D. M. Brinton (Eds.), *The content-based classroom: New perspectives on integrating language and content* (2nd ed., pp. 67–78). Ann Arbor: University of Michigan Press.

Short, D. J., Fidelman, C. G., & Louguit, M. (2012). Developing academic language in English language learners through sheltered instruction. *TESOL Quarterly, 46*(2), 334–361.

Snow, M. A. (1997). Teaching academic literacy skills: Discipline faculty take responsibility. In M. A. Snow & D. M. Brinton (Eds.), *The content-based classroom: Perspectives on integrating language and content* (pp. 290–304). White Plains, NY: Longman.

Snow, M. A. (2014). Content-based and immersion models of second/foreign language teaching. In M. Celce-Murcia, D. M. Brinton, & M. A. Snow (Eds.), *Teaching English as a second or foreign language* (4th ed., pp. 438–454). Boston, MA: National Geographic Learning/ Heinle Cengage Learning.

Snow, M. A., & Brinton, D. M. (1988). Content-based language instruction: Investigating the effectiveness of the adjunct model. *TESOL Quarterly,* 22(4), 553–574.

Snow, M. A., & Kamhi-Stein, L. D. (2002). Teaching and learning academic literacy through Project LEAP. In J. A. Crandall & D. Kaufman (Eds.), *Content-based instruction in higher education settings* (pp. 169–181). Alexandria, VA: Teachers of English to Speakers of Other Languages.

Snow, M. A., McCormick, J., & Osipova, A. (2017). Academic language across educational levels in content-based instruction. In M. A. Snow & D. M. Brinton (Eds.), *The content-based classroom: New perspectives on integrating language and content* (2nd ed., pp. 270–283). Ann Arbor: University of Michigan Press.

Song, B. (2006). Content-based instruction: Long term effects and outcomes. *English for Specific Purposes, 25,* 420–437.

Spring, J. (2010). Sustained content-based academic English teaching through paired English and philosophy courses. In J. Nordmeyer & S. Barduhn (Eds.), *Integrating language and content* (pp. 219–230). Alexandria, VA: Teachers of English to Speakers of Other Languages.

Srole, C. (1997). Pedagogical responses from content faculty: Teaching content and language in history. In M. A. Snow & D. M. Brinton (Eds.), *The content-based classroom: Perspectives on integrating language and content* (pp. 104–116). White Plains, NY: Longman.

Stoller, F. L., & Grabe, W. (2017). Building coherence into the content-based curriculum: Six Ts revisited. In M. A. Snow & D. M. Brinton (Eds.), *The content-based classroom: New perspectives on integrating language and content* (2nd ed., pp. 53–66). Ann Arbor: University of Michigan Press.

Tan, M. (2011). Mathematics and science teachers' beliefs and practices regarding the teaching of language in content learning. *Language Teaching Research, 15*(3), 325–342.

Tedick, D. J., Christian, D., & Fortune, T. W. (2011). *Immersion education: Practices, policies, possibilities*. Buffalo, NY: Multilingual Matters.

Townsend, M. (2001). Writing intensive courses and WAC. In S. H. McLeod, E. Miraglia, M. Soven, & C. Thaiss (Eds.), *WAC for the new millennium: Strategies for continuing WAC programs* (pp. 233–258). Urbana, IL: National Council of Teachers of English.

U.S. Department of State, Office of English Language Programs. (2007). Bilingual primary. *Shaping the way we teach English*. Washington, DC: Author. Retrieved from http://www.youtube.com/watch?v=caOXPCIGFyM

Valeo, A. (2013). The integration of language and content: Form-focused instruction in a content-based language program. *The Canadian Journal of Applied Linguistics, 16*(1), 25–50.

van Lier, L. (2005). The bellman's map: Avoiding the "perfect and absolute blank" in language learning. In R. M. Jourdenais & S. E. Springer (Eds.), *Content, tasks and projects in the language classroom: 2004 conference proceedings* (pp. 13–22). Monterey, CA: Monterey Institute of International Studies.

van Wyk, A. L. (2017). Content-based instruction as a means of addressing linguistic diversity in higher education: A South African example. In M. A. Snow & D. M. Brinton (Eds.), *The content-based classroom: New perspectives on integrating language and content* (2nd ed., pp. 178–190). Ann Arbor: University of Michigan Press.

Wesche, M. B. (2010). Content based second language instruction. In R. Kaplan (Ed.), *The Oxford handbook of applied linguistics* (2nd ed., pp. 275–293). Oxford, England: Oxford University Press.

Wu, M. H., & Chang, T. M. (2010). Heritage language learning and teaching through a macro-approach. *Working Papers in Educational Linguistics, 25*(2), 23–33.

Zappa-Hollman, S., & Duff, P. (2017). Conducting research on content-based instruction. In M. A. Snow & D. M. Brinton (Eds.), *The content-based classroom: New perspectives on integrating language and content* (2nd ed., pp. 309–321). Ann Arbor: University of Michigan Press.